Teaching Father how to Impregnate Women is an intellectual property of its author Soonest Iheanyi Nathaniel with exclusive publication rights owned by RLFPA Editions (OPC) Pvt Ltd—an imprint of RædLeaf Foundation for Poetry & Allied Arts, not-for-profit, independent literary organization committed to promoting poetry and allied arts in India and abroad. Since 2012.

ISBN: 9788193929513
First Edition: Dec 01, 2018
Cover Art, Design & Layout: Linda Ashok
Funded by: *RædLeaf Foundation for Poetry & Allied Arts*
        as a part of RL Poetry Awards winning series.

TEACHING FATHER HOW TO IMPREGNATE WOMEN

Poems
by

SOONEST NATHANIEL

Winner of
RL POETRY AWARD 2017
(International Category)

CONTENTS

Preface

Preface

Through the ravaging curse of colonialism, breaking through the ashen grounds of death and destruction, acquired cultures arose out of the inflicted that went on to assume definitive shapes over the past century and more. Of these *outgrowths*, perhaps the most elitist and powerful was literature, born in the Anglophone, Hispanophone and Francophone voices of the most oppressed and their progenies. It happened in virtually every acre of all continents, Africa being one. Seventeen African countries became independent from British rule in 1960, Nigeria being the most populous. While many illustrious pens have embroidered Nigerian literature written in both English and native languages at continental and international levels since the country's independence fueled by internetic openness and unlimited access of global resources, the new millennium promises to append to it a plethora of rich creations. One such creative voice sprouts in this book with the veracity and intransigence of a defiant stem.

In *Teaching My Father How to Impregnate Women*, the bold and vernal voice of Soonest Nathaniel launches in his otherwise traditional narrative poetry an offensive—transgressing, mocking social norms, systematic suppression of sexual openness, exposing the reader to a split spearhead of wit and cajolery. With a vocabulary rich and wide, that underscores the need for a new language, Soonest wields his prose-poetry flute to charm the magical–lyrical to his beck and call. Although working within the bounds of traditional narrative poetry, the poet is able to build a signatorial voice through a carefully chosen vase of interesting image-associations often making room for shock & surprise wherever and whenever possible. Although the witty title of Nathaniel's book and the false-façade of many of his poems tend to both mock the cultural primitives of "manhood" and fakes misogyny at times, at its deepest core his poetry salutes the empowered woman. In a poem titled "It doesn't take a penis" the poet talks about a mother with odd fondness-

> *I was born by a woman, who sits like a man.*
> *Her legs wide open without fear*
> *for what the prying world would see.*
> *And she will say,*
> *'let them bear witness*
> *that this lady is endowed with an elephant-size testicle'.*

Nathaniel puts his delicate, caring finger on the perils of gender misidentification, ritualistic oppression of male-centric cultures, the organized scrutiny of the ever-suspicious margins, the onslaught of death and abundance of blood on all roads leading to the expression of innate freedom. Twinned with his rich language, Nathaniel frequently uses intertextual devices like unnamed quotes with judicious economy.

Welcome to a new and powerfully promising aperture on Anglophone African poetry.

Aryanil Mukherjee
Cincinnati, USA
November, 2018

Aryanil Mukherjee is an Indian-American poet and editor of *Kaurab*, a literary journal. He was the judge for the foreign category of the RL Poetry Award 2017.

vi

TEACHING FATHER
HOW TO IMPREGNATE
WOMEN

Fetching the Rains

My father fears to watch his children take to the road,
he fears he might enter a world of metaphors.
He is married to the night,
but I am a bat in love with the dawn.
Father's limbs have grown heavy,
but there is fire in my feet;
I can hear my heart dance to the music of my thuds,
my journey began where his had ended.
Last night I took to the road,
on the path out of the village I met a cat,
but I did not heed its warning;
for life is worth nothing
if not lived in curiosity.

Father says the world is flat,
he warns that I might fall off its tapered edge.
But I say,
'when doves shed feathers off their silver wings,
I will glue the feathers together and take flight'.
I tell him I will touch down on the other side,
where seagulls skim over the waves.
Father says sometimes the road turns to water,
and I say
I will grow fins,
I am not afraid to drown;
for this child must learn
to father himself.

I tell father
I know of dead villages,

I know of cremated hopes,
but I do not know of dead roads.
I want to gather new stories,
for a village where peace has died away
like a cigarette in an ashtray;
I go to get new stories,
for a house that lies full,
reeking of tales which lips fear to tell.
I do not long to inherit my father's gods and concubines,
I depart to find a new name.
And when I return, I will come with the rains
to wash off our roofs, the corpses of dead narratives.

It Doesn't take a Penis

I was born by a woman, who sits like a man.
Her legs wide open without fear
for what the prying world would see.
And she will say,
'let them bear witness
that this lady is endowed with an elephant-size testicle'.

My mother wears yucca fibers for sandals
and rabbit furs for clothes.
Her neck is adorned
with shells, stones, bones and dried berries;
and she will say,
'dead memories too are ornaments.'

On certain days
she will place my head on her thighs
and with affection in her eyes
she will say,
'big ships drown in pools, ponds and puddles,
 it doesn't take a penis to impregnate a woman'.

So at the school of her lap,
I learnt to castrate my fears
in faith to fertilize the womb of barren dreams.
Last night I heard her say,
'the open road never dies,
it leads to a lake full of laughter'.

The Garden of Earthly Delights

Paint a portrait of innocence
for Dante and Virgil in hell.
Tell of the death of Marat;
head severed.
I watched Saturn devouring his son
and Judith decapitating Holofernes,
the grim handmaid.
The beast of the sea
makes merry,
celebrates the temptation of St. Anthony.
Mask this still life,
for the fruit of death has been planted
in the garden of earthly delights

Through the Back Door

For Mansir, whose identity was mistaken

They will let you out
through a dark corner,
after putting you in spaces
you do not inhabit,
spaces you would never occupy.
They will let you out
Mansir;
into a virtual space far from home.

They will let you out
into a world of questions
and like an equation
the world will ask you D-y?
It's a stupid world created by a genius called god.
The dumb population wielding smartphones
will ask why you painted your nails,
why you wore Barbie's clothes,
yet come with a factory fitted penis.

They will proffer exorcism,
from the spirits,
the bad spirits that inhabit you.
They want to rid you of spirits averse to conformist ideas,
spirits that cause you to crave a walk off the tapered edge of the
flat earth;
yes, their earth is flat.
They will let you out
Mansir,
into a world without pencils to line your eyes;
they don't want you to see ghosts.

They will let you out
into darkness,

into a rigid world of roles and rules,
a world where dogs have more rights than men,
where god has made it all and there is no room for creativity.
They will let you out
Mansir;
and no one will apologize.

They will let you out,
set you forth before dawn,
when the day is neither black nor white;
Perhaps maybe when the skies are grey.
They will lead you through a corridor in the courts,
after the judge has found in you no flaw.
They'll walk you through the blue door,
disappointed that they cannot sate
the mob's thirst for blood anymore.
They will let you out
Mansir,
they will;
but only through the back door.

Parting Ritual

When father died,
they shaved my mother's head
to the scalp,
then they forced her to bath
with the algae-green water
gathered from rinsing father's corpse.
Six yards of white cloth
sewn into a mourning gown,
mother wore a smile,
it was more lethal than a frown.

They forced her to eat,
they said she will need strength,
strength to look the dead in the eyes
and confess to lies,
lies that she ate her husband and his other children.
Hers was a feast of worms,
and though sadness filled her stomach,
she struggled to eat the maggots
wriggling from the ears, eyes, mouth and orifices
of delayed justice.

They let her walk the meadows on barefoot,
father's grave had been dug at the end of the groove.
They claim she crossed the thin line
between apples and snakes,
so at the nodal where two positions meet,
she will light seven candles,
then circle the grave with chalk.

For 90-days,
they confined her to a room,
the 'other room',
where every limp comes to pose as a patriot,
where every screamer thinks himself a prophet,
and every crook claims that he is a statesman.
But after all the lechers and mourners go home,
my mother will rise and make love to silence.

Symbols

for Omran Daqneesh

Dirt and blood form a patch on your face,
the failed job of a poor cartographer
seeking in his own faulty map
a place where peace can be planted.

Hairs fall over your brow,
like a hut losing its thatched roof
to a nasty storm.
Our house is on fire.
If we stay, we burn.
If we leave, we drown at sea.

Yesterday,
My brother was on TV.
They say his face has become a controversy.
They claim his looks are an excuse
to invite the devils.
But how do we get to choose
what symbol we will eventually become?

Yesterday,
along the streets to our house,
there was a boy lying on the floor.
His legs were missing.
I heard they didn't want him to walk off
the tapered edge of our flat earth.

There is a mother who will never know sleep again.
The cartographer placed her home on a field filled with mines.
A father cries shamelessly.
They gouged his daughter's eyes out.
They say she had seen too much.
They claim she had seen the nakedness of God.

I am almost home.
The air is thick
with the stench of death.
I have come to collect the pieces of the people I love.
I have come measuring distance in silence.
I've come to keep the corpses quiet.
I only hope that my shirt won't pass
as a symbol of infidelity.

I Smell Death

I smell death.
I tread on blood.
I am last on the procession line;
the last line of code.
The light has come and gone.
The programmer will never return.

Some dreams die before they are born.
Arrows in flight never return.
So I ask:
'Who writes the algorithms of our fate?
Who plots the graph of our existence?
How can we measure our lives in binary?'

They aimed for his head,
lodged lead in the nursery of his brain,
and they found out
he did not bleed in pseudo-codes.
His mnemonics had their binding time.

They have come again.
They always come,
assemblers,
compilers
seeking to decode the language of memory,
daring to dissect destiny.
They ask: "When is the end of eternity?"

And some long for a look into the infants' eyes,
longing to read the past of tomorrow;
yearning to know the future of yesterday.
When flowers grow teeth,
Lord, let my flesh not pass for meat!

Who will write the Messiah's iteration?
Who will program the day unknown,
now that the light has come and gone
and the programmer will never return again?

Calculus

We solved the differential of our existence
by counting small stones;
but they said
the depths of our minds were way too shallow.
Their analyst said we needed precise axioms
to capture the ghosts of departed quantities,
so they plotted our lives on their X-Y charts.
Their palmist read geometric woes
from the lines of our palms
and said:
"This is the limit to which your fish brains can function."

But I ask,
who gave them rights to run evaluation
and pose theorems of existence?
Who gave them the impetus to fix yardsticks
and set standards of living?
Who said we are but indefinite integrals
and who made them higher order derivatives?

Oh, tell them!
Tell them we know,
we know there is a rate of change,
we know the vicious circle is bound in continuity.
Tell them we need not their almighty formula
to solve the equation of our utter confusion,
tell them we can fix our stochastic systems
and can find the roots of our own identity.

Yes tell them!
Tell them we shall cover the erotic distance
between dreams and reality,
when speed and time share
a sweet romance.

Mystery of the Five Houses

I
At the house of light bulb,
there is fog.
The man with the child in his eyes
has a cat which sits daily on his lap,
gazing constantly at the big sky,
searching curiously for Peter Pan.
In the warm room,
the Lord of the Reedy River sleeps.
Under the ivy,
The handsome cabin boy sips
his cappuccetto grosso.

II
At the house of silence,
they pose riddles
that only the dead can answer.
The grave robbers
do the dance of the dogs
before unearthing secrets.
The wolf and the raven
play the peacemakers
in a debate over greed.
No evidence against the black sheep,
the alibi pans out,
and again the tomb becomes a womb
from which the fetus of truth is aborted.
The dead pity the living,
as slaves beg for the cadavers of other slaves.

III
At the house of leaves,
the roads fall out of the windows.
the decomposing trees make for bridges,
bridges over the gulf of ignorance.
The children of rain
join the roots to their school,
underground.
Their chlorophylls have been extracted,
they cannot carry out the photosynthesis of their existence.

IV
At the house of jealous lovers,
the keeper of storms
opens the floodgate,
and the rooms overflow
with the rage of angels.
The weather is an equation,
the weatherman altered the arithmetic,
and the victims of mathematics
are stranded.
There is no sailing away
on the ship within the bottle.

V
At the house of memory,
there is a shrine of madness.
Pieces of glass litter the floor,
there is a song on the lips
of the broken china.
The clock has lost its limbs,
no one remembers

the dance steps
to songs of the season;
the world is ill,
she suffers from future syndrome.
Dead children smile
from wind-kissed pictures.
There is a woman left brooding
upon the ledge,
it's the gravedigger's wife;
her lover is coming home tonight,
he is coming to attend his funeral.

The Pulitzer

Life on Mars
the best of it
is only an abundance of nothing.
So we took core samples
from middle-earth
to make beds for trees in the sky.

At the tryst of failure
we watched the shadow of Sirius
shatter the glass of human innocence
and dismember the limbs of time.
We watched the native guard
inseminate an elephant
and make love to his late wife.
Still watching the spring festival
of delights and shadows
there at Martha's Vineyard,
we found out what love comes to.
Who would have thought
that Moy sand and gravel
were the makeup of practical gods?
They say each one lives for different hours.

At the republic of poetry,
we encountered a blizzard of one.
Dean played an elegy on toy piano
and from the black zodiac
sprouted an orchard;
O! The dream of the unified field,
American sublime.
But eye-shots don't tell the simple truth,
so we learnt to speak the neon-vernacular.

In the before life,
they say we were wild irises,

thank goodness for near changes,
the metamorphosis of the wild.
The world doesn't end,
thus never give partial accounts
till you have heard from the other lover.
O! that I understood the mystery of small houses.

Blessed are they who can see
their full self-portrait
in a convex mirror,
the transparent man too
is made of flesh and blood;
eats bread and drinks wine.
Saints and strangers make promises,
not of things of this world,
but of the waking and dream flights.

Preach
strange holiness:
salvation for flowering stones.
Grace:
feed slaves on meat
and sons on cornhusks.
Faith:
these new believers
must take the old road to paradise.

Fulfillment

Fulfillment is the smile
his mother's corpse wore today.
The moon on this eve of her funeral
has entered that phase in which it becomes a door,
door into a history class where a boy has raised his hand
to ask a question about motion.

They say cows do not speak, but this son is no cow.
No! This son is no cow,
this son is that proverbial donkey
whose eyes have been blessed to behold an angel.
He has been taught another way.
This son knows the world is vain,
he also knows that dirt can be made holy;
so he never mocks his own vagary.

He walked into the history class
a man dressed in women's clothes.
His masculinity gentle,
His femininity strong,
His arguments weighty;
and he would say,
'Who cares if the prophet hangs himself in disbelief?
Fiction will always tell a truth that history can never
comprehend.'

How to Leave Home

If you must leave,
then let it be on the most quiet night,
when the roads have been deserted
and there are no dogs barking in the distance.

Be certain the streets are naked
before you venture into the un-fabricated dark,
into the valley of discolored bones.
Be quick on your feet,
but do not let your ears hear your thuds.

A bevy of bats will flap through the reeling dark,
you must not bend your head,
you must not fret,
even as the darkness threatens
to swallow your resolve;
just mutter your mother's name beneath your breath.

If the crickets are silent and the frogs are quiet,
and there are no fireflies;
light a lamp in your heart,
let the wick be made from passion.
When you meet the cat, do not stop.
Do not entertain questions from strangers,
do not answer familiar calls.

At the crossroad,
you will be tempted to look back, but don't;
not because you are afraid of mutation,
but because you do not want a loved one's kiss
to lure you into changing your mind.
For you must go to fight the bloodless war,
and then you must return with the golden sword,
to bring to an end the shaman's monopoly.

She knows the Road

She knows the road out of the village,
out of the maze of our dark history,
out of this box with four sides
closing in at right angles.
She knows the road
to that place my father is afraid to name,
that place where the earth is a sphere.

She knows the road out of the 'other room',
out of the cage filled with children
who bear ancillary dreams.
She knows the road out of spaces with accidental geometry,
there where the forgotten children are forced
to understand public grief,
yet the children still laugh at their father's funeral.

She knows the road out of the desert of memory,
out from the grave of the womb;
away from this place where the earth died screaming.
In her eyes lay the compass.
In her eyes lay the map.
In her eyes lay corridors to cities of desires.
But my father does not love her,
he says her mouth is full of her own stories.

Harami

Sometimes she gets sweet-
stories of ice-cream,
those eaten by children
of strangers.
For her, it is sacrilege to dream
of green wheat fields,
the orchards
 and vines
pregnant with plum grapes;
those planted by fabled poets,
the odes cultivated to appease
their wanton lovers.

She did not choose to be born
this way,
feet first;
beloved daughter
of a rejected mother,
honorable mention,
consolation for a virgin
desecrated and shamed.
But here she was,
mouse living in a rat-hole,
situated in paradise;
fed fat and fresh on crumbs
of milk biscuits
and legally stolen cheese.

To love a man
her mother says is to hate yourself,
but what is woman
without one to take her as a book
off the library's dusty shelf?
Sometimes she wonders

how bad it is to dream
of being held in the firm arms
of a father, brother, lover;
to be sang like some sweet psalms,
to feel the caress of warm palms
upon the petals of a rose.

Someday she wishes to bear sons,
she longs to kiss their lip
and hold them tenderly in her grips
as maidens cling to their urns.
But until then,
she must make do
with the stories of ice-creams,
those eaten by the children of strangers.

July's People

If only you had seen this place
moment before the house-gun went-off
and life became one death race;
there was no place like it.
You should have seen the town
and country lovers
trailing Friday's footprints;
you would have loved to come again tomorrow.

Once upon a time,
just before
the jump,
the loot
and other stories;
there was an occasion for loving.

It was before the lying days,
before ours became a world of strangers.
Then when our dirty linens were not for publication;
the world wanted to hear my son's story.
Not of sooty escapades on the mines,
nor of lifetimes under apartheid,
but of the Burger's daughter.

There was something out there
for July's people.
It was not just the essential gestures
of politics and places,
but that was till we met the wily face to face
and enrolled in his correspondence course,
just to keep our idle selves busy
and say something for the time being.

But who would have remembered

that Beethoven was one-sixteenth black?
Maybe just a few of us,
the black interpreters;
we who after the first cycle
became the conservationist.

And these days,
some would say to us,
'please go-get-a-life'
claiming we are in a new era,
and we will often reply,
'what new era would that be?'

N/B: Lines from this poem are drawn for the titles and phrases from Nadine Gordimer's vast oeuvre

Personal Demons

coalition of the unwilling

At noon
we bury them
in the arch of our smiles,
Only to have them resurrect
at night,
walking the horizons of our eyes.
They said it was wrong to turn right,
they say all truths are well coined lies.

Which shore is spotless,
Which war is bloodless;
Which!
Even those without guffaw
leave sores that the needle can never stitch.

Indeed we fought,
At wee hours,
At odd hours;
Before
the wick of faith went out
and the darkness of doubt lurking
by the door
took over our hut.
No shore is spotless!

The far right and far left
increasingly agree (to hate)
and old allies claim innocent bystanders,
but what can be innocent about apathy?
They end up adding their loud silences
to the seemingly cold violence;
and even the deaf can hear their dumb screams.
Every war is pointless,

nightmares also have dreams.

No war is bloodless!

In a quest to sate our righteous hunger,
we go poaching in the wild;
illegal harvest of ghosts.
We seek to defaunate the world of shadows.
Some didn't want to be kept,
but they didn't want to be thrown back either;
Liberty too is captivity.

Spotless! … Bloodless!

Teeth
and tongue
quarrel over who can taste better
the steaming song.
The lover longs for no tomorrow,
on his bones the mushrooms grow;
In the bride's heart hate grooms,
hope is a suicide rope.
We acquaint ourselves with our demons,
hang new believes in old shelves;
Ours is the coalition of the unwilling.
Thus the bullied and the bribed
must savor life's unripe lemons
till that which was never lost will be found.

No shore is spotless
No war is bloodless
No war
No!!!

These Corpses must Speak their Names

for the bodies found floating upon the Ezu river

They have bobbed-up belly-wise,
like fishes drawn out of water;
there's a message in the white of their vacant eyes,
and we are left the riddle to decipher.

The river does not swallow what she did not chew,
so she has rejected them like the fart from a harlot's anus.
We who watch them lifelessly float drown internally,
as we drink the scene with voracious thirst like famished camels,
and let the message of fear written on their faces
sink effortlessly into our minds like stones.

Their adept and inert swimming skills we gloat,
those autonomic reactions, those untrained eyes;
their rather calm behavior,
it all smells like foul play.
So we ask,
were they passive or active in this strange task
of burying themselves in a watery grave without a coffin?

We question the corpses to explain,
but amnesia they feign.
The doctors claim they have suffered great hypoxia,
the matter is sapping, spent is the oxygen in our brain.

But on this issue,
sleeping dogs will not be left to lie.
For our sons are no bastards,

only young prodigals that have forgotten their fathers' names.
There's a vasoconstriction restraining the flow of truth in their
stiff veins,
but today the tree shall be known by its fruit.

Though they deprive us of oxygen,
still we shall have our justice;
for no fragrant perfumes will hold back
the stench oozing from their orifices.
These corpses must speak their names.
And though they char their remains in capricious flames,
still we shall attain the open secret,
from the lips of their ashes.

Rhetoric of Redress

Rend the veil of silence
with the bleating of the lamb,
the price is paid;
the slain are the victors.

Blood stamps
on our door posts,
let death's angel pass;
we are reborn.

Let the rum red sea
return to her forlorn bed,
baptize Pharaohs
who won't set us free.

Freedom they say
is a life sentence,
yet give me cyanide
than have me forever enslaved.

I stood between death and the seven pillars,
Passed the four walls, entered the circle
and through the blue door;
headed for the kingdom in the sun.
Home of the damned,
the let downs
the hopelessly hopeless
and the not good enough.

Sing no more about the rain,

for losing all doubts is freedom.
Fear is all buried alive by time,
So we look forward to new hard times.
We are at our worst, yet we won't yield;
for we are too young to kneel.

Cathedral of Vain Desires

There is a tale floating in the murmuring tide,
a sad song riding aloft the raft of wind.
It is the story of a savior nailed to a wheel,
a tale of the rage and rebellion of angels
at the theatre of salvation.

Ours is the kingdom of madness,
some drunk on the latter rain,
others perfecting the art of telling lies;
sorrow is the flavor of the day.
At the house of mirrors
is a new profound fear,
our faith must walk bare-footed on broken glass.

We are deathly little dreams,
flies in the eyes of the queen;
we are unbelievers
who must take the short walk
down the long hall to redemption.
We seek the land of miracle,
thus we must go night swimming in the deep end.

With blood we erect a house for God,
a god so blood thirsty, a god so flesh hungry.
Who said we can't pay our way to heaven?
Who said we can't buy our way to salvation?
There is no sin too dirty to be washed away,
there is no crime too weighty to be forgiven,
not when love is a liquid.

But our Lady of annihilation is unforgiving,
this mother is merciless,
she eats her own children;
so when the princes of death come,
stringing Kalashins
like guitars and violins,
then both saints and sinners
must savor the dark symphony of the vain glory opera.

In the russet gold of this vain hour,
the altar boy kneels with aluminum stilts,
and on the wings of a dream
a heartfelt prayer stands.
The candle of grace is frozen,
and in vain repetitions,
we seek for a trace of life.

Casualties of Mathematics

I

They are the millions intimidated by language,
those who linger in the shade of Galileo's labyrinth,
all in a failed attempt to escape the burden of interpretation.

Victims of chromatography,
they do not know what to do with sunlight.
Their chlorophylls have been extracted,
they can no longer carryout
the photosynthesis of their existence.

II
They are the myriads of idle hands praying
to a drunk god,
seeking to rouse a slumberous yard
into a rhumba of rattling demons.

Pawns of prophecy,
mortal-gods captured at the dawn of creation.
Watch them veer off course
in a futile bid to find themselves on the frame of reference.

III
They are the children of chaotic situations
those caught in the crossfire,
searching for a distinct heaven
away from the scourge of racial purity.
They have no one to sympathize with them.
Oh! What pain to watch them trying in futility
to grapple the language of rejection.

Stepmother Said

She said the sentences of her life keep missing their periods,
a lecher suckled at her nipples before she grew breasts.

She said: 'your father thinks there are boons and bounties
at the boundaries that circumference of my areola, he thinks
there are prophesies to be fulfilled at the nodal of my pudenda;
but that workman is always at war with his tools.

'So he lifts my skirt over my face and shows the world my
shame; but bastards too have surnames. The weaver weaves lust
into baskets to bear his bounty of disgrace.

'If only your father could weave his women like he does his
baskets, then maybe someday, their wombs will hold waters,
hold sons and daughters.
'Boy never forget that humans too are pliable.'

Reflection at Baby's Clinic

The year the rice crop failed in my homeland,
father took a third wife.
She was full Indian, knew the rope trick,
could turn water into wine.
Like all true daughters who walk this path,
she believed in breaking all the rules.

I saw her once undressing,
taking off the clothes that escaped 67.
I was peeping through the square window,
her body a new galaxy, and her eyes led to a world elsewhere.
So like a robin in flight, I bade farewell to my father's earth.

Reader I tell you, this is not another fantasy
of an African boy having the window dream.
I was in love and it did not matter
if she caused the death of Richard.

And the world said we will be stranded at baby's clinic
but here now we are, Ruby and I at the lab,
the experts agree with the midwives of the spirit,
they can all hear a heart-throb,
they can all feel the foetal-kick
 in the navel of the soul.

The Basket Weaver

A woman weaves baskets in Cameroon,
for grass she uses boy's pubic hairs
and for rush, the thicket of their eyelashes.
She twines into wicker baskets,
men's beards and moustaches,
and stores in her womb
beer,
grains
and the skulls of decapitated dreams.

She sings as she does here weaving,
her song says hope is reed
which forms the spokes and staves
of ambitions without base.
It says lust and greed are weavers
to fill the insides of nothingness.
It says sweet lies are peddled best
on the lips of 'honest men'.

She chants a savory song,
the fools ear refuses to eat.
it says love is cocoyam,
patience is oil;
and all you require
to enjoy this meal,
is to sprout again your milk teeth

Before you make love

'Get drunk on snail semen,
and learn to do the dance of the whooping crane;
Enact the established rite among Staffordshire figures
and paper-mâché reveries, with the detached formality of
nightmares

Circumcise your heathen self and ingest your foreskin,
cut lengthwise all the way to the scrotum,
drip the blood over the fire of your longing,
urinate from the underside of your penis
not your urethra.

And while you play bison in Hayden valley,
remember,
before the sperms erupt,
like magma from the groin of a boiling earth,
you first must establish her cycle.

So learn to
Count her heartbeats
Till the 25th hour of the day,
Till the 8th day of the week,
The 5th week of the month,
The 13th month of the year;
Son,
never forget
that good loving
may take a light-year-of-darkness.

Evolve

After Langdon Smith

When you were a centipede,
I was a millipede.
I bet our difference was time,
distance or maybe length and speed.
Maybe
you measured in centimeters
while I did mine in millimeters;
but all we trailed was one lead.
Phylum 'Arthropoda'.
You of the tribe 'Chilopoda'
I native of the 'diplopoda';
Ever creepy ,
ever lovely,
critters, lovers.

Unconsciously we lived,
Unconsciously we loved
and unconsciously we died.
We slumbered side-by-side,
Groom and bride;
by the flames of passion engulfed.
Time turned on the lathe
And we spun by the tools of fate,
into some other entities shaped.
Unfortunately, we hadn't lips to debate,
but luckily, we begat breath
again in the womb of death;
Where again you were my mate,
though now to a higher echelon evolved.

Now to phylum mollusca,
we took life slow and steady,
crawling tenderly upon our belly;
still then, you were my only lover.
O! How I loved your lips
and its gracious offer of hydrocolloid-jelly;
the doting nectar.
You snail, me slug,
creeping slowly, softly, gently;
to meet, meat and mate upon the grassy-rug.
Change remained constant,
but didn't come instant.
Once you were a tadpole,
I was a fish;
then we became amphibians
against our wish.
Together toad and frog,
two unknown aliens.
The hour-glass turned,
we died once more.
Again though we returned,
meeting by the Specton-shore.
This time we had scales and tails.

Gleefully we lived,
Joyfully we loved,
Happily we died.

Our forms translated upon the Putton-bed.
Our eyes opened at dawn
and we noticed we bore the traits of the bird.
Feathers and wings,

and the hands that did us make,
did also in us embed,
a fount from whence sweet songs spring.
Then each one
flew-on,
free-to-air,
here, there, everywhere.

Liberty besotted our heads,
we should have, but we were never wed.
We pitched our nest wherever we deemed best;
not for a moment pause to think of the other's interest.
Sometimes, I wish I could reinvent time,
then we'll go back,
down the Darwinian-track,
to when we were creepy-lovers,
lovely-critters;
but the clock of change stopped,
and we are stuck with these wings and feathers;
from innocence to impudence,
evolved…

After making Love

After making love
we hear footsteps,
familiar thuds;
bodies entwined,
souls departing down the hall.

They say the bed is a battle floor,
children spoils of the war.
There is something romantic about a lover's snore,
but who goes to sleep
while strangers guard their door?

So we hire a goldsmith,
take the lavish gold
out of the empty bags
and weigh the silver in the balance;
we make idols.

Love makes men afraid as grasshoppers,
so at noon we make noise like dogs
going round about the city;
and at night we make our beds to swim
and water our couches with tears.

In dreams
we bare the legs
uncover the thighs,
pass over the river,
but there is no one to answer when we call.

She left
and Eden became a wilderness,
no tree to be desired to make one wise,
we die to make old friends,

we kill to make peace.

Light so bright
it becomes darkness
the diviners have been made mad.
We drank of the wine,
we drank from the prophet's skull.

Make crowns of thorns, Jesus will die twice.
Lay her, that perfect sacrifice
at the altar of fame.
We'll make God in our own image,
we want him to change, we want him to feel our shame.

A Note for Small Mommy

The day I called you mommy, I knew like the 3-year-old boy in primary who won't let his mother leave for work, that I won't leave you, I knew like that boy I will wait brilliantly in class, half the time relishing the joy of a mother's warm embrace; and my lust will fuel my legs ready for that race into your arms again after the closing bell of joy is tolled.

Do not fall asleep mommy, do not drift as I tell you now the tale of a boy whose eyes were always on the clock, urging it to tick away the light of day, to that time when he like a sheep long gone astray may return to his mother's fold.

And the world will wonder how he passed his exams, but who will tell them that at the school of his mother's thighs, he often recalled in love all he had learnt only just to behold the smiles on her face and the glint in her eyes.

Who will tell them that for every correct answer, he got a kiss, and often some dry fish to show he scored a great point.

Small mommy, I am that son, who would outpace lightening itself, just to be next to you, with palms stroking my hair, while I purr lost in your care

Nne, I am that boy who your love made into a man never afraid to cry, who learnt from the slate in your eye, that for every woman loved, the earth finds another reason not to dry up and die.

Mommy, the day you called me daddy, tears seeped through the crevice of my heart and welled in my eyes, for I knew that the baton had been passed from girl-to-woman that this child who must father the man must drink his childhood; to womb dreams whose reality the world earnestly awaits.

Adanne, I knew that in the school from which graduation is impossible, I had found a teacher, whose motherly care will keep me in class; I won't be shy to show the world my report card, for you score the sheets, and love is the pass mark.

Loving Women Day-by-Day

Sunday's woman makes up to entice angels.
Her smiles are titillated spells,
and her hair is a collection of hymns.
She is clad in fabrics of goodness,
and in her pot, a cauldron of courtesy steams.

Monday's woman does not cook breakfast.
She wakes before men's alarms,
before the cocks crow.
She hits the road very early
to watch empires rise from her cup of coffee.

Tuesday's woman takes neither tea nor coffee.
She misses the 6:30 bus
because she had to do yesterday's chores.
She fixes a quick meal for her husband,
tasty goodness with little salt and pepper of course.

Wednesday's woman wears baby pink.
She needs to look as cool as she can
before the probing shrink.
Bitter with the mirror's judgment,
she asks her blind man 'Honey, what do you think?'

Thursday's woman always has a bible class,
her skeptic husband calls on the Rev Father
and Father says there will be no further mass.
He gets home decades before her,
and by 10pm, she's by the door,
preaching triumphantly

that Jesus rode on a donkey not an ass.

Friday's woman drinks rum.
She sits by the bar all night,
waiting for a date who never comes.
She won't have herself stood-up,
so she orders for two and asks herself to a dance.

Saturday's woman longs for her wedding.
She is a virgin and cannot wait for the first night
when she will taste of the pudding.
But last night her groom fell in love with a stripper
at the bachelor's eve.
He says "Who cares about weddings when one can attend his
own funeral?"

The Women We Loved

The women we loved
loved other men,
my mother
so engrossed with her man
didn't nurse me on her breast.

She'll rather not have them fall,
she'll have them stand tall;
ever ready to heed and answer
when he calls.

But that
which the toddler's tongue
didn't do,
time did;
its hands fondled her wilt,
and the lecher
her milkman
sought fresh udders
in Sarajevo.

So I turned to my sister,
but she had no breast;
and there was nothing we could do,
on the day she was spoken of
and given to a man
who has a vagina between his thighs.
I tried to turn to aunty,
but she asked me to look outside the tribe.

So these days
I have learnt to look elsewhere
and there to live with the scars of light.

The Mute Witness

for Narendran who lost Chandrika

Last night you vanished,
now I see you
in many places at once.
I can't believe it,
I am confused;
wondering whether to protest
or be hurt.

Life too short
to linger,
too fast
to move on.
I am learning to keep pace
with the light and the swift.

We planned to bake dreams,
cake them into bricks
to build a paradise
high up
the Nilgiri hills.
But it's become hard to get your attention.

I hold no grudges,
I have only lost all expectations.
No memory
to bound me to the past,
no faith
to capture me for the future;
this atheist has got a god,
my religion is unbelief.

The potted plants are pale,
no one shows them sunny love
anymore.

The cat has grown skinny
I have nurtured her
on the milk of melancholy,
she feeds daily on bad poetry.

She still walks with grace though,
still winks when your portrait smiles.
I have put my life up for rent,
my soul is left at auction.
Give away clothes,
give away shoes,
give away identity;
the world has suddenly grown too big,
I am trying to make it shrink.

We can rearrange furniture
but not our lives.
The shelves hang askew,
the books have lost their jackets.
moths and maggots merry in our kitchen,
the rodents have seceded,
they have taken our room.

One stool sits
out of place,
and even strangers can tell
that home resides here no more.

N/B: Written in conversation with Moni Basu

Not Alone

1.
I still do not know what you found
when you looked through the windows of my soul,
into the hull of this sand castle.
I wonder if what you found
was just my fear, or the truth
about how women become leaders.

2.
You say you will stay
through the storms,
I say it leaks through the thatch,
but you remind me,
we cannot leave
saving the plants to the environmentalists.

3.
I say it's a season of grief,
you ask me to savor the salt
and see through the tears.
You say we must learn to walk the wilderness,
by seeing the world through the eyes of Abrahams
who never cast away their lots.

4
I say I cannot see through silk to silicon,
I say I cannot see through the eyes of innocents.
But you say I am a marooned child at the shoreline of time,
searching through the eyes of Katrina.
You say I must learn never to rush through the early days of
childhood,
so I am learning to see through the crack, I am learning through
vanishing point, the essence of space.

5.
You ask what I see through flowers,
I say I have never seen through the eyes of an artist.
I ask if you could have your baby
through egg donation,
you say it's all anemophily,
your pollination is through the air.

6.
Nne, my doctor who sees life through the patient's eye,
my teacher who teaches maths through nursery rhymes;
at your foot I am learning to appreciate the music.
With the dog's ear,
I am learning to hear God through the noise.
I will convert myself through hymns,
I will forgive my sins,
for through your eyes, I realize that I am not alone.

Never Dies

She was awake all through the night,
her orgasm was a fake.

Like the fisherman, he denied
when she informed him of her pregnancy.

He asked her 'by whom?'
He asked her 'with what?'

'Putrid prophesies, catholic curses
and beautiful blasphemies,' came her sultry reply.

She said she was pregnant with stocks for Shylocks,
she was pregnant for a merchant who trades dearth in season
of harvest.

There was no milk from her breast
on the day she returned with a chick to their nest.

So he said he would put litmus to test
to affirm that her lies were corrosive.

He said he would have been deceived
if he accepts her and her child.

He won't be fooled
to accept her 'lies too sweet, supple and poetic'.

But the feces he refused to earth now gather flies,
and the scales begin to fall off his fickle eyes.

The fruit has pointed to the tree, from which it fell,
and now he seeks to find that which was never lost.

He forgets,
that which never lived, never dies.

Lustre

There is a lawful woman in a bad place,
she has been taught
that sin can be irresistible;
she is hooked on the spice,
found the boy with a problem,
their romance has grown from a whisper to a scream.

Life is sweeter when tasted on lemon tongue,
lust is a hot potato soup
served best on the radical history of love.
On the other side of midnight lays a miracle,
but it is a crocked pathway to paradise,
whoever said it is always sunny in Philadelphia.

We try luring our demons to sleep
by telling them the story of a squirrel,
but in the sullen world of broken hearts
there are tears before bedtime, tears on the sheets,
monsters under the bed, monkeys dangling from the ceiling;
it is hard to keep your arms steady, pages waver like black sails
in the sunset.

In the dowsing hour of the troubled night,
a still voice rings like that of a familiar spirit,
it says beware of the doves in snakes clothing,
beware of false messiahs, pregnant virgins and temple
physicians;
beware the bone diggers who can only live the day you die.
Remember, monkey schemes are best applied in periods of
grace.

Bubbles

The promises in your eyes have been replaced
by a history of hate,
righteous-hate for a lover who got lost trying to find himself.
I watch helplessly as stones boil in your disappointed heart.

As the sun goes down, traditions end.
I watch you consume different cultures,
the world has been fed poisons.
You paint on your shabby bed, pillowcases pass for canvass.
Ink splattered all over, by the corner your doll is looking for its
head.

History is inverted.
Brilliant obituaries pose questions,
you are thirsty for answers,
but your daddy's mind is a well welling unwittingly.
He is trying to reboot his memory, trying to format his mind.
I fear he won't be ready before this city begins to have sex with
itself.

Dark Black

for Achalugo

In the swamp where alders grow,
the girl with invisible sun in her hair
plants follicles of hope.
Between darkness and wonder,
she charts a new course
for spirits in the material world.
She believes celestial navigation
can be taken on domestic fuels.
Far from the country,
bridges burn
and angels
are yet to mend their differences,
but the dove in her heart
sees no reason to lose sleep,
it hangs on to the moon,
gathering small twigs,
pine needles and cattails,
certain it will build a home of dreams,
for every little thing this girl does is magic.

From a Prodigal Son to a 'Pius' father

Father, I have chosen for myself a simpler name,
one which the birds can easily remember,
something sweet like Michelangelo.

Don't worry,
this bastard still has a surname,
I have only just erased daddy's little defects.

Here
in this strange land,
patients prescribe drugs.
So doctor, here are my prescriptions for your disease.

I know you think men must grow leather tough skins, you
blame women for their children's sins.
You are an oracle too sacred for poop and piss,
if only you knew the grace of a smiling baby's kiss.

I know you fear to dance naked,
you won't even take your shoes off
before getting into bed.
You think she will assume
you are weak and vile,
but who said men don't cry.

Congrats! I heard your wife is pregnant
and she is observing lent.
You think perhaps if she fasts a little longer
her baby's sex will change.
So I write to inform you,
even dolls now come with a factory fitted penis.

Father, you must Learn

You must learn to write love letters,
poems with living verbs,
verbs fragrant like the farts of morning flowers,
flowers planted over living men's graves.
women love to drink lost vowels
and missing alphabets.

Father you must learn,
you must learn that lions too can be gentlemen;
so crimp your claws and lose your teeth,
let your tongue lose like a hound
in wild search for that mellow song,
fast breaking,
fading,
fading away into the woods,
into the deep dark night
of her inner-tans;
remember though,
we can't find God through the curves of women's bodies.

Father you must learn,
you must learn that gentleness is no weakness;
thus, learn to let her love you like a child,
for in the winter of life,
when all vigor seems lost in the limbs of the zestful clock,
it becomes common place to have a shriveled cock.

If I were to Meet my Dead Father

If I meet him by the baobab tree
which sits at the center of the road to our village,
I will stop by, sit with him a while
and listen to the frogs in furrowed concerto.

When the choir hushes its singing,
I will take my father up on that debate
regarding the occupants of the 'other room'.

I will argue the negative.

I will say,
to win the nectar of the flower
you must be a butterfly not a bee.

I will say,
women are not always ripest in winter
and the best things in life are still free.

I will say,
women's ears eat more than honey
and their eyes sulk more than milk.

I will say,
father you must return,
you must return,
if only just to witness
how wild cats can feed fresh and fat on legumes.

The Tailless Cow

The cow they bought for my father's funeral was nothing like him. Gentle soul it was, sat still beneath the odara tree at the Centre of our family compound.

They bought a cow without a tail. Perhaps, all the money father had saved-up in his pillowcases were not enough to purchase better cattle. And the children gathered around it, watching flies buzz about its eyes and buttocks; waiting to see God chase the flies away.

When the children had run out of patience, and God was not forthcoming, they began to chase the flies away themselves. Soon, it was time to kill the cow. The elders gathered around the tree and watched without remorse as the butchered severed the cow's head.

All through the process, the bovine was calm and pliant, it did not sob so much. The children watched the entire time, they watched the tailless cow beings slaughtered and shared by my father's kinsmen. Some watched in excitement while others watched in disbelief.

For the latter that were yet to lose their innocence, I wonder if they felt sad that God did not lift a finger for the tailless cow, I wonder if they wished like I did, to see the cow put up a good fight.

But there we stood and watched helplessly, even as father's kinsmen shared the boons of perverted justice.

Remind Them

I was chastised yesterday
because I couldn't recite a salat.
I did not cry,
but there was blood
gushing from my mother's eyes.
She wasn't there, but could feel it,
evident were the stripes upon her flesh.
There was ice in her stomach.

The handwriting was on the wall,
and though stack illiterate
she was,
still she could read it all.
Hers' was a lesson
of the corpse after decay.

My father recites a Maghrib
at dawn,
they said their act was a Dhikr,
Oh! These things we do
in remembrance of God.

Today,
I joined the roots
to their school underground.
Already I have learnt,
that which was never lost cannot be found.
I have lost my doubt, now faith i hound.

Laughter still lays hostage at Westgate,
if only we could buy sorrow's cure at the mall.
Beware sons who laugh
at their father's burial,
for children know more about public grief.

The sunset has changed mother's color,
the rains have come late;
the sea still streams from her eyes.
She recites in Norse a Nicene creed,
chants aloud canticles of the sun.
Buried on her lips is the litany of saints,
her chaplet is soaked in blood.

Faintly now I hear father say:
'Remind them, Oh Allah!
remind them, that peace also is halal'

Mystery of the Fishmonger

for Mouhine Fikri

Bouazizi's ghost is thirsty.
His soul longs for a spring.
He walks barefooted
along the streets of Al-Hocein.
He is looking for that oasis
where men deprived of justice
may sate their thirst.

He finds an inert body
along the deserted path.
It's that of Fikri, a fishmonger.
Fikri's head and arms stick out
beneath a lorry's crushing mechanism.
Bouazizi's ghost is scared,
but he won't run,
for he can relate to the scene,
he who was an actor in a drama of similar fate.

Bouazizi can't find water, so he starts a fire,
and stones gather in protest,
all fishmongers in their own rights,
they whose driftnets bare boons of swordfish.
For some, their trade is illegal,
so they'll have the fishmongers' wares destroyed;
but like the man in the lorry,
these fishmongers will throw themselves in after their fish.

The bridge has been burnt,
and the citizens can't find their way

back to the state.
The season is ripe for the harvest of broadbills
in Casablanca and Marrakesh,
thus silence is forbidden
on the lips of bitter fishwives.
Like Bouazizi's ghost, Fikri's has stirred a wildfire,
and Rabat can only hope that Sebou's plea can douse the
flames,
before the walls begin to close in for an incestuous romance.

Madagascar

Beneath the amazing looking baobab trees of Madagascar
are scars of swollen trunks,
trunks of sapping scorn.
These upturned trees
give bread to monkeys;
leaving the children of men unfed.

As slender as the baobab is squat
So are the dachshunds;
Who too often settle for the simpler name
"Weiner dogs".
These badgers hunt the critters
that live deep in the tunnels
of our long forgotten island.

We enjoy a long neglect,
this neglect will test your spirit's yield ability;
and when your soul's resolve
encounters the yield sign
while driving along Kowalski street,
then you'll be forced to ask if you truly do exist,
or if your existence is yet another unverified myth;
Here, even gods from their pre-occupation resign.

We play the hopscotch with destiny,
sometimes scratching-off
the thick lines of fear
that dares us to win
in this game of life.
Our life is a soft riddle,

a succulent proverb, a mellow paradox,
whose tough literal meaning is a distraction
designed to keep one from seeing plain things in sight.

The gardeners of faith
prune ideological youngberries,
those hybrids
possessing the grafted beauty of blackberries,
the pruned rascality of raspberries;
and the spliced doggedness of dewberries.
These hexaploids of faith
concocted in the womb of necessity
gave rise to the invention of our vegetative-democracy;
this they say is one side of the divide,
the seers say that the answer to the riddle of our uncertainty
lays on the next slide.

And between the baobabs, dachshunds, your yield ability,
hopscotch and our youngberries,
if you ask me what secret meaning ties them to this Madagascar,
I'll tell you I'm just as dumbfounded and share your
uncertainties;
For the answer obviously is nothing.
This nothing is the new pod of valid hope
on which we hopelessly grope.

We have Come

a found poem

We have come home
to the gathering,
to share the inheritance of loss.
We are they who live the life of pi
and only believe in the god of small things.

We have come
via the needle's eye
to sew a stitch in the fabric of time.
We are they who ply the ghost road
where the phantom of Paddy Clarke silently screams.

We have come,
Lazarus' from the dead.
Take away these grave clothes!
We are they delivered of old devils,
Bone-people come to savor the remains of the day.

We have come
with songs of the waves
and the rattle of pebbles on the shore.
We are midnight's children
observing the rites-of-passage.

We have come
for the loved ones and the left alone,
the marooned at the siege of Krishnapor.
We are the conservationists
sailing offshore on Schindler's ark.

We have come
for the one and yet repeated time;
kindred spirits, refusing to stay-out by the baobab tree.
We are natives of trouble,
peacefully seeking a good name for bad sleep.

How to Return

Returning is a skill
you won't acquire on history class,
a skill I acquired at my mother's laps.

My mother said:

If you must return
with the tides,
then let it be
in an upturned canoe,
down the meandering stream.

Mother said:

If you must return
with the winds,
then let it be
on the silver wings of doves.

Mama said:

If you must return
at the nick of night,
then arm yourself with a machete
blunt enough to clear the forest
of it's macro-stench and venality.

Nne said:

If you must return
at dawn,
then seal your lips with a reed,
for the smoothest of journeys
are those undertaken in silence.

Symphony of Dreams

On the outskirts of town
lies a spoonful of dreams.
At the crossroads,
the troubadour will find
the true shape of things.
I'm on my way,
they say love is spreading
over the world.
I listened to the radio,
they say clothes don't make a man,
so I go naked
to the old town
to fetch a bowl of summer sunshine;
to begin again.

Dreams call out to me,
they call me into the ocean
of your smiles.
Love is a lonely harbor,
regrets are ports;
but this is no song for injured love.
This is a symphony of the forest,
the wayfarers passage to life.
The masquerade is over,
tonight is a moondance
at the garden of remembrance.
Tonight is for wandering of the womb,
for walking the clouds of unknowing,
for seeing with broken eyes.
Tonight,

the cursed,
withering and wishing
shall gather fragments.

I'll sing for dinner,
savor a drop of silence,
and drink the midnight mist,
for I know the solace of shadows.
Tonight is for fleeing the bloodlust,
to plant a seed in the womb of fertile fantasies.
Tonight,
 I go,
searching,
seeking,
reaching as always;
tracing back roots,
of fire,
        flesh
            and bone.

I've been around for too long,
so no asking from broken statutes,
no looking into mirrors,
I'll find directions in your eyes.
Tonight,
we dance.
We dance
to the symphony of dreams,
we'll let the music set us free,
so at dawn,
we can sleep,
when we are dead.

A Young Poet's Prayer

When time like light goes out of the corridors,
and darkness fills the passage of love,
let me be able to boast of not merely sitting enthralled
to gratify the elders.

Let them say they were perplexed,
let them say they were vexed
to have their youth avidly recalled;
and when compared to mine,
theirs a share waste of bustling energy.

Lord! I do not long to end up like them,
old men who are nobody's uncles;
those fishes which nobody wants
with their chips.

True, a man cannot be a messiah forever,
but these men have delivered no one,
not their households nor themselves;
maybe a few wanton women.
Now the room is cold with old age,
and all we can say of them
is, 'Oh they used to have their grandmother's smiles'.

Vanishing Point

I have watched my uncle crumble and become fragments,
he prays time hastes away, he wants to run out of memory.
My uncle says he failed to embrace stubborn dreams of
perpetual energy;
he will leave the world without delivering power to the touch of
the teeming millions.

The old soldier listens keenly while the Atlantic replays the
philosophy of the sea.
From his balcony he can see the waves,
eyes fixed like an old poet waiting for his young lover surfing
upon the tides;
but she has strayed too far into the offing,
there is no returning from the place where the sea kisses the sky.

The coffee spills in his shirt,
and he asks me to help him take off the regalia of his worried
mind.
He says to me 'boy do you know when a man drowns himself,
we do not bury him in his father's compound.
We leave his body in the forbidden forest
and hang his head on the poles used to mark boundaries.

'The people watch as days run into years,
and soon they begin to harvest honey
from the hull of the deceased's skull,
where a swarm of bees have settled in the hollows
and made honeycombs.
Boy it won't matter what names your fathers bore,
for the hunger in the eyes of the disappointed, knows nothing
of honor.

When I Returned

The forest was slumberous
and the lake was almost dry.
The rains had all gone on exile
so no one remembered the dance of the seasons.
Our village was I'll, she was suffering from
backward syndrome.

The living still saddled themselves
with keeping the corpses quiet,
the dead were yet to find rest
in the people's memory.
So I began to teach them
that letting go is a new form of love.

Our young ones had no love for books,
very few took to reading,
the shelves were filled with works
which have long gone out of print.
So I built them a new library,
taught them to read stars
and to read geometric progress
from the lines of their palms.

There were old men
still trying to see the robed world
through the gods' naked eyes.
At the prayer ground,
the women looked up at the rolling sky,
seeking the seventh proof.
They got stuck struggling to grope on loss,
holding on to nightmares.
It hurt me that they were fighting to keep their sanity,
it hurt me that they were fighting to prove their existence.

My mother ended her age long romance with silence,
the victim quit her job as an accomplice
to a crime she knew nothing about.
She took off her mourning gown
and invited the griots.
They sang in praise of the troubadours,
they sang in praise of the road.
And while they sang,
the rains returned from their long exiles,
the rains came flapping through the yard.

When I returned,
my mother walked out of her grave,
she danced with the children in the streets;
they danced to the music of the rains.

I Am

I am the sore tale
of the prematurely ruptured hymen,
the bitter, aftermath stale taste
of a lustfully decanted semen;
I am an African child.

I am the last echoed note
of a sweet, faded song.
The empty can's music you loathe,
the blank message of the rattling gong;
I am the African child.

I am the skeleton of a dead dream,
the eclipsed flux of the moon's beam.
I am the cadaver of addle visions,
the remains of rotten aspirations;
I am the African child.

I am the special gift of the bowels of fate,
the best offering from penury's greatest estate.
I am the fume of smoking factory chimneys,
the chime of the poor beggar's pennies;
I am an African child.

I am the content in the belly of the ashtray,
the lesson of the corpse after decay.
I am the uncultivated alluvial core,
a virgin maid that's known no man ever before;
I am an African child.

I am the spot of the leopard,
a sheep straying without shepherd.
I am a candle light hidden under a bushel,
an innovation trapped in ignorance's cell;
I am the African child.

I Write Programs

iterations of change

I write programs from the pseudo codes-of-silence,
generated in those graveyards where dead gods are replanted.

I write programs whose mnemonics have no binding time,
whose lines are un-decodable by mere mortal memory;
nor compilable by any system software in the annals of history.

I write programs that divide and conquer all problems,
altering all inclement weathers and averting natural mayhems.

I write programs whose commands draw rains in seasons of
drought
and cause vegetation in arid deserts to sprout,
availing bread and grain for the seething starving mouths
of African women and children
dying of want, though they dwell in the heart of a fertile Eden.

I write programs, a bubble sort of algorithms
that harvest diamonds from the eye of the alluvial sky,
to foot the bills of the poor beggar's dreams,
giving rejected cornerstones the wings to fly.

I write programs that debug our failed systems
of virtuous viruses and presidential parasites
embedded in the bloodstreams and marrows of our society,
My programs feast on the cadaver of mundane polity,
devouring the souls of those children conceived of ill-fated
technology.

I write programs that detonate the tinkling bomb of fanatic
apathy,
by defragmenting the bias and prejudice of tradition, religion
and education,
Software that plots and executes coups
to unseat avaricious kings of democratic-anarchy.
Routines that arrange in arrays the sins of the treacherous
fathers,
fixing them in a linked-list and linking their punishments to
their treasonous sons,
even down to their unborn generations of cabalistic offspring.

I write programs that make extinct our dirty past,
make obsolete our mediocre present,
and out-date our confused future.

I write programs from the pseudo-codes of silence...

The Series

Fibonacci wrote a series,
from zeroes of cosmic ages,
the primordial androgyne,
the plenum.
Down to the ones,
the glyph,
the monad, the yang;
the hidden intelligence.

Then the duos of alteration,
Of diversity and conflict;
the hypocrisy of mankind.

Followed closely
by the triples, the triplets, the triune
and the threefold existence.
Technology keys-in on 3D,
the dimensions, their stems rooted in multiplicity.

The triad
and the tripartite nature of the world.

After we pass the three phases of the moon,
the genies asked us to make 3 wishes
and we watched as upon the tripod
the mystery of alchemy was unraveled.

The fourth dimension is an illusion,
solid in a very liquid form;
do not roll the empty drum.
The four cardinal points,
gear forth the four winds,
blow forth the four seasons,
interactions of the four elements;

Air,
    Earth,
Fire,
    Water.

We drank from the four rivers to paradise,
those before Eden's premature demise.
The Euphrates,
Pishon,
Gishon
and Tigris.
We trailed their banks,
seeking-to-find the shell
of the human microcosm; the quincunx being.

We trailed the fire pointed star
and the fire petaled flower of quintessence.

We applied the sixth sense to equilibrium.
From the duodenum of the Orion,
we awaited the six rays of solar's emergence.

We learnt that the earth daily boils and rages
but the answers to the problematic equations
have been put forth by no sages.
And though scholars will traverse on Odyssey voyages,
though seekers will roam through the seven ages
of man;
still,
no one can unravel the mysteries.

So
Naaman
has to deep seven times,
preach this prophecy to the seven churches,
for soon the waves of the seven seas will surge.
The plagues of the seven broken seals shall be open to men.

We will build a temple
on the pattern of the Mandala
to attain the eight chakras.

Lend a life
from the nine
of the feline,
the cat's wife.

Pull death by the ears
and ask him;
'Don't you realize
that we are the paradigms of creation?'

Prepare for rebirth.

The Decalogue
is the map,
break one rule
and you head straight for the morgue.
Odysseus must now return,
Troy has fallen.

There'll be no eleventh commandment
for the twelve tribes of Israel;
and to these laws,
there will be no further amendments;
wisdom is folly that seems right.

Eureka!

My mother holds regular debates with Newton
beneath the apple tree.
Free spirit
she knew nothing about gravity;
she won't be pulled to the earth,
her children's ambitions were reason enough to defy dogma.

Life had always tried to submerge her
wholly or partially in mud, urine and feces;
but she remembers there will always be an up thrust,
so she displaces her fears and acts in the upward direction.

She knew only the righteous blind with see the rising sun
at midnight.
So she kept trying to inscribe spheres within cylinders,
kept trying to make perfect circles of every given triangle.

Always solving for the exact number of cattle
in the herd of the sun,
always counting the number of grains of sand
that will fit inside the universe.

She will say: "we must acquaint ourselves
with the objects of our fears,
we must look the worlds in their eyes
and say to them 'do not disturb our circles'".
Mother will always remind us
that though our hopes dangle
like the testicle of the pendulum clock,
still there will be sweet-marah

from the eyes of the crying rock.

The day after her last debate with Newton,
I decided to creatively forget to dress,
I decided to consciously unmask myself.
That day, I hung old skins in new shelves
and ran into the streets shouting Eureka!

I knew my mother had finally won the debate,
I knew she had to leave for she was fulfilled,
she was convinced that she had taught her children,
the Archimedes of existence.

The Kitchen

These days it is deliberately kept dark and silent,
the broken teacup
still sits near the empty sink.
I open the refrigerator
and instead of food,
It is stocked with debts,
and bills and suits.
There are grey bowls
in the orderly cupboards,
but they are filled with nothing.

I am hungry,
but no gas to start a fire,
the kettle is dry,
the tap is thirsty;
I would give my little finger
to hear again the applause of running water.
This used to be a room where music was cooked,
then when it belonged solely to my mother,
when she would bake the world for me
while I vamped on the imaginary piano
my father etched on the kitchen table;
and the fridge would always hum
like a chorister with helpfulness.

The dishes are clean,
the drawers are locked.
Father would not allow anyone open it,
but I am no more that child in the man's eyes.
so I pull them open like a mortician,

secrets lay lifelessly on the platter
like corpses in the trays at the morgue.
I unearth the secrets; they are quite simple and domestic,
They speak of those times
when there were always shards of broken innocence littering the
floor,
I remember those times when the cats would tirelessly chase
shadows;
I want to raid this kitchen and rid it of those unearthly hours.

I begin
by pouring
the remaining smudge of regrets
out of my grandmother's jug
into the patched sink,
then I fill the grey bowls in the orderly cupboards
with the blood of berries, grains of laughter
and the essence of sublime moments.
This kitchen must return to being the room where music is
baked,
this glass of silence must be broken by the applause of running
waters.
I will fill the gas and fix myself a pot of coffee,
I will give my left eye
 just to watch kingdoms rise again from my mother's teacup.

Interpreters of Nightmares

Into the eyes of the hunter
they go excavating the earliest ideas.
They go seeking the buried goods,
the family silver,
and all things tangible
that linger on the threshold of illusions.

Seers of the spirit,
they walk with the golden key in hand,
opening doors to unknown worlds.
For them, it is more than a family affair,
more than black magic,
more than animal magic.

These custodians of the blueprint written in stone
were born to birth civilization out of mud;
their history is the Torah
written in the wind.

They bear the course of work outside the sacred garden.
While the Shepherds are drowning the deer,
they are keeping watch over the flocks.
They have found a way to conquer death
by travelling back to the future;
they do not travel on borrowed fool's gold,
for they know the world is an illusion.

Yesterday they stood on the promontory of Asia
and called the sun out of its grave.
Tomorrow they shall renew the social contract

between self,
             state
                  and society.

They shall retell
the horrors of the past fight,
the terrors of the present
and usher in
an age of diamonds.

Acknowledgements

Some of the poems here have appeared in slightly different versions in *Rattle, Pedestal Magazine, Elsewhere, Loudthots, Scintilla, Northridge Review, Praxis Magazine and Raven Chronicles.*

Many thanks to Dami Ajayi and Adeola Opeyemi for taking out time to read earlier drafts of this manuscript, their insightful takes and edits added to the shaping of some poems within.

The title of this collection and a few of the poems here, were written in conversation and in standing-in-spirit with Warsan Shire; for people who are generally not heard.

That said, I dedicate this book to Promise Nathaniel and Brigitte Poirson, my mother and my godmother respectively; the greatest believers in my art; women who deserve more appreciation than they have ever gotten.

Soonest Nathaniel
Agege, 2018

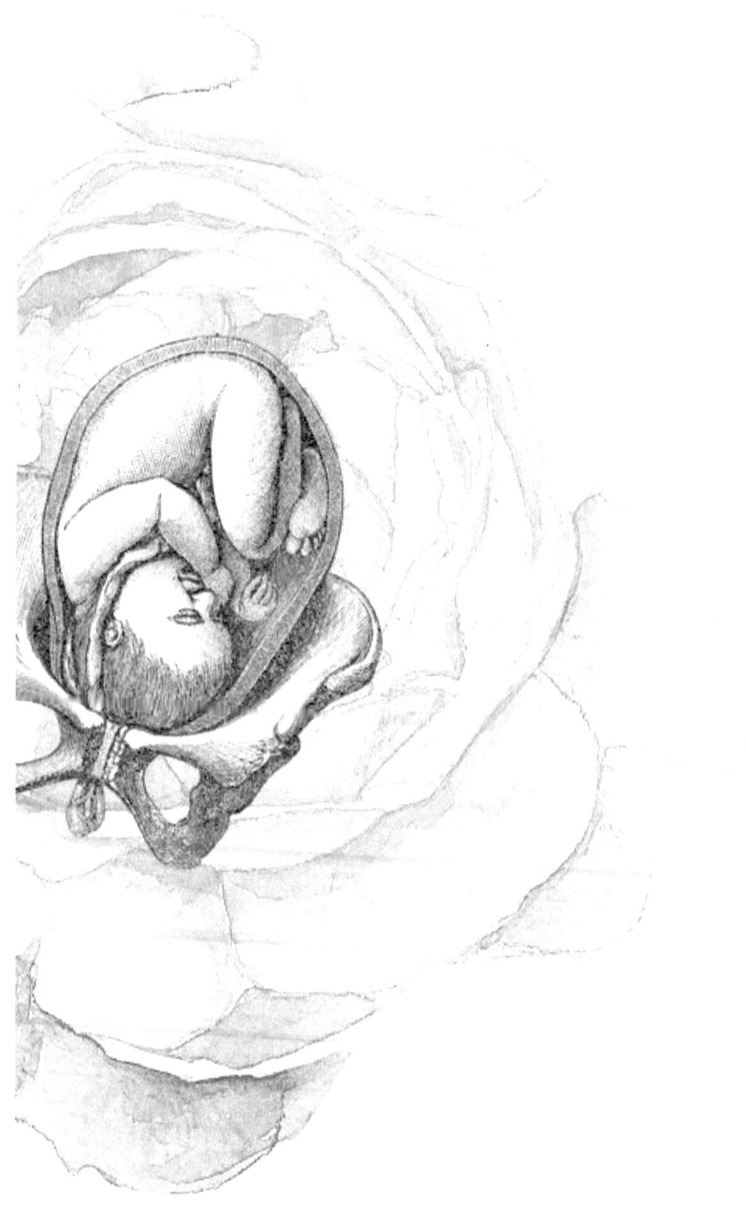